# Franchising Steps to Success

A guide designed for business owners thinking of franchising their company now or in the future.

Ian Stirling

**Franchising Steps to Success**
**Copyright ©: Ian Stirling**
**Published: 1 July 2012**
**ISBN: 978-1-291-61388-9**
**Publisher: Ian Stirling via Lulu.com**

All rights reserved. No part of this publication may be reproduced, stored in retrieval system, copied in any form or by any means, electronic, mechanical, photocopying, recording or otherwise transmitted without written permission from the publisher. You must not circulate this book in any format.

**Business advisers and consultants can obtain a PDF version that can be provided to their clients, on the understanding it is provided totally free of charge. It must for provided in full without any additions, deletion or changes.**

# Contents

| | | |
|---|---|---|
| Chapter 1 | Franchising your business | 4 |
| Chapter 2 | Businesses suitable for franchising | 7 |
| Chapter 3 | Common questions from prospective franchisors | 9 |
| Chapter 4 | Franchising support for business Owners | 14 |
| Chapter 5 | Franchises work | 20 |
| Chapter 6 | Franchising is not a miracle cure | 22 |
| Chapter 7 | Traits of a successful franchisor | 23 |
| Chapter 8 | Franchise types | 25 |
| Chapter 9 | Selecting franchisees | 28 |
| Chapter 10 | Recruiting Franchisees | 32 |
| Chapter 11 | Marketing your franchise | 35 |
| Chapter 12 | BFA approval | 37 |
| Chapter 13 | Franchise documentation | 39 |
| Chapter 14 | Start at the beginning | 47 |
| Chapter 14 | Now you can make it happen | 52 |

# Franchising your business

Firstly, it is important to understand franchising. A franchised business is when a business owner (franchisor) sells someone a licence to set up a company which will trade as a branch of the franchisor. The franchisee (this licence holder) has to use the franchisor's brand image, business systems, keep to its philosophy and market the franchised branch as if it was part of a chain.

Each franchisee runs a separate company or business. The best franchisees for most businesses are people who wish to be their own boss, but are looking for a proven business model, with support, so they start earning a wage quickly.

The franchisee buys the franchise or licence. The fee paid for this would normally cover the franchisor's costs for setting the franchisee up in business.

The franchisee pays the franchisor a monthly fee based on one or a combination of:

- percentage of turnover
- mark-up on the goods or materials, that are normally purchased from the franchisor
- agreed fixed amount per month.

These amounts are paid for the full term of the franchise agreement.

Franchise agreements usually last for a minimum of five years. Renewal of the agreement should usually be straightforward, provided the terms of the agreement have not been breached.

The most important aspect of becoming a franchisor is to make sure you protect your reputation and brand. This is achieved by producing a very detailed operations manual that covers everything that should and should not be done. People are surprised that it covers minor items like when to clean the van or shop, however it is important to remember that most franchisees have never run a business and will have many demands on their time.

For example, the details in the marketing section could include instructions that state that the franchisee must allow half a day per week to make 20 telephone calls to potential customers and connect to 10 businesses on LinkedIn. It is this detail, and the management of it, that has made franchising so successful.

Many people think of franchises as being major brands such as, McDonald's, Burger King, Molly Maid, Prontaprint Dominos Pizza, Dyno-Rod, Global Travel, Pizza Hut, Bairstow Eves (estate agents), Clarkes Shoes, Subway, Toni & Guy (hair dressers) but there are many more smaller franchisors. Some franchisors have 4 to 10 franchisees and are not looking for more, as they still wish to be hands-on in their business, rather than becoming merely a manager of franchisees.

According to the NatWest Franchise Survey, which uses a very strict definition of franchising, there are 897 franchisors. However, there are many more franchises with less formal licensing agreements.

## Businesses suitable for franchising

The business must be making a profit after paying anyone who works there, including the owner. The franchisee will need to generate enough income to pay all their costs, including a salary for themselves, plus be able to pay off the cost of the franchise over the five year term.

The business does not need to have been trading for more than a couple of years, however do consider the following points.

1) Is the business profitable after adding back the costs of tax, depreciation, loans and personal expenditure?

2) Is there a demand for the product or service nationwide?

3) Is the owner willing to invest in growing their business and do they have £2,000 to £5,000 cash available?

It costs less to franchise a business than to open new branches or employ staff. However, it will require an investment of cash and time to expand any business. In the early years the franchisor will normally make less profit, per branch, with franchising as they will be sharing the profits with the franchisee. In later years increased volume and scale are likely offset this, and larger businesses can be created from re-investing the income generated by the franchisees.

In practice, it takes most business owners 12 months before they see a real ROI, (return on investment). This is because the documentation and franchise package has to be created before a business owner is ready to promote their first franchise. This can take 4 to 5 months and some businesses need to develop their branding or systems. It might take a little time to recruit the first franchisee because a new franchise cannot supply references or show their business is working as a franchise.

## Common questions from prospective franchisors

- **I have competitors, some that are franchised. Is there room for us?** Most businesses that have a large enough market to support franchisees do have competition. You are successfully competing in the market place now, therefore so can your franchisees.

- **Do I have the skills to manage the franchisees?** Before franchising a business, the owner should seriously consider having an independent review of their business carried out by someone that understands franchising. During the review any professional franchise consultant should discuss what is involved in managing franchisees. If the owner then decides that they need assistance in managing franchisees, there are businesses that can assist them by providing both management and/or administration support for their franchisees. The cost of this support can often be built into the on-going franchise fees.

- **Why do I require an independent review of my business, as I know it works well as it is?** There are a number of reasons. One is that the way someone runs their business today might be different from the way franchisees ought to start a business. The business owner will have learnt many lessons since the day they started the business, so it is not normally sensible to start a franchise in exactly the same way as they started the business. Also, a professional with franchising experience will often assist the business owner to simplify the franchise offer. Business owners often wish to add as much as they can into the franchise offer to make it look attractive, however, in many cases it has the reverse effect, because the franchisee sees it as a more difficult franchise to operate.

- **Will the franchisee leave and take some of my business?** Firstly, remember they will be tied to a contract for five years. If after five years they are successful, they are likely to renew their franchise. If they are unsuccessful, even with your support and structure, how likely are they to survive on their own?

- **How long will the franchise agreement be for?** Unless there are very specific reasons for a shorter term, the standard is five years.

- **How big should territories be?** Business owners spend a great deal of time on this question. However, it is not that important when the first franchisee is appointed. It is better that the first two areas are generous, as it is vital that a franchisor starts with successful franchisees. This approach also rewards those franchisees who support the business owner in the early stages of franchise development. The territories can then be mapped once experience of franchising has been gained.

Some franchisors are looking to grow their business so they mainly become the manager and trainer of their franchisees, whereas others wish to continue with the hands-on management of their core business and provide support to their franchisees in a different way.

It is possible to franchise a business that already has a branch network. Once the franchise package has been created, the branches of the business can be sold off as franchises with existing customers and trade. This can make them popular.

Another successful option is to have a mix of company-owned branches and franchises.. It is important that the franchisees are treated fairly, when measured against the company-owned branches.

## Points to consider

In practice, the biggest risk to achieving any ROI when franchising a business is spending time and money partly preparing the franchise package, but never completing it. The main reason business owners do not complete the franchise process is that they believe they can create the business reviews and documentation in-house. They then discover they do not have the time or just get bogged down in trying to understand the franchise process.

Also, when a business reviews its internal systems, it can always find things it would like to change and dealing with these leads to delays and costs. An independent franchise expert would only suggest changes that matter to the franchisor's business or the franchisee.

As it is difficult to look at a business as an outsider would, internal reviews seldom really question processes that are completed a certain way from habit. Therefore they miss simple changes that could easily be streamlined, particularly as far as the franchisees are concerned. For example, with changes in technology, it could now make sense for franchisees to report or place orders using mobile communications.

To sum up, it is important that a business owner understands the amount of work involved in franchising a business before they decide to proceed. Every owner should ask themselves if they are going to pay someone to produce the documentation and, if not, whether they are willing to spend their evenings and weekends writing a business growth plan and the detailed Operations Manual. The owner will also have to allow time to produce, or have produced, franchise marketing materials, as well as time to interview and answer questions from prospective franchisees.

# Franchising support for business owners

## Using a franchising consultant

The advantage of using a professional franchising consultant is that they will have documentation that is common to most franchises, which can be used as templates. Normally over 50% of a Operations Manual is standard text. The parts of the manual that are specific to the processes carried out in operating the business are the sections which will take the consultant the most time to produce.

A good consultant should not only have a great knowledge of running a business, they have to be able to relate this to running a franchise. Most consultants will meet with a business owner without charge to gain knowledge of the business. It is important that this is a two-way process, so in return the consultant will receive the opportunity to promote their services. Even at this first meeting, a professional consultant can show they understand in general how they would franchise the business. This would be by giving advice on the types of franchisees that are likely to be attracted to the business, suggesting what will make the franchise stand out and showing how they would use their sample documentation.

The consultant is unlikely to leave sample documents if they own the copyright on them, as they will have taken many months to create and perfect.

Some consultancies own franchising magazines or run franchising shows. It is important to make sure that any consultancy deals are not tied to selling other services. The consultant should have one goal – that is to make the business successful as a franchise.

## Points to consider

It is important to know who will carry out your work. It might be that you will meet with a consultant who creates notes on your business, which are then passed to a draftsperson to produce the documentation. Alternatively it might be that a team creates the Operations Manual and a marketing team handle franchise recruitment. Some consultants will work on your franchising project handling both the meetings and the creation of the documentation.

Consultants that share some of the risk, by deferring part of their fees until the first franchisee is recruited, will have a greater commitment to the process. The best contracts are created by both parties sharing at least some of the risks and equally some of the rewards.

It is important to agree a schedule showing when payments for services are due. The standard is normally 50% on signing and 50% on receiving the documentation. Some consultants will agree to 40% on signing, 40% on completion of the documentation and 20% when the first franchisee is recruited. If the consultant is confident the business model is correct, they are only delaying receiving part of their payment and this arrangement shows that they are committed to franchising the business, rather than just producing the documents.

Again, it is important that the owner understands the total commitment required to franchise a business. Consultancy fees range from £5,000 to £50,000 depending on the size of the business and the complexity. Many consultants have a minimum price of £20,000 to £25,000, therefore a business should work through the franchising process with the consultant to make sure the entire process, with the exception of legal work and advertising, is included in the fixed fee.

Some consultancies offer lower rates if the business complete 50% of the documentation. Before anyone accepts this route they do need to assess their skills and availability of time. Do discuss in detail what is included in each 50% section. It might be that the time-consuming parts which are specific to the business are the owner's responsibility and it is the consultant's role to produce the more standard business information sections. It is true that the business owner will have a greater knowledge of the business operations, however part of the value of the consultant should be their independent insight into the business.

If a £20,000 fee is beyond the owner's budget, look for smaller consultancies, where the owner can be more flexible and will negotiate a rate between £5,000 and £10,000. This is a less suitable option for franchises that require a large investment by the franchisee, as the banks might wish to see the name of a large, well-respected consultancy, on the feasibility study before lending. This is less likely to be an issue with lower cost franchises.

**The DIY option**

If a business owner with limited or no experience of franchising starts to create a 'franchising package' with a blank sheet of paper, it will be hard for them to get the franchising structure correct. They might think they have considered everything and they are confident that the manuals and procedures are correct, however, issues normally arise when the legal agreement is created. This is particularly true where an experienced franchise solicitor is appointed. Much of the legal agreement is written to enforce the Operations Manual to the word. If items are missed out of the manual or are too vague, the legal cost can escalate or the business may not be fully protected.

If a solicitor has doubts about the completeness of the manuals they are likely to advise the owners to have their complete documentation reviewed by a franchise consultant. The cost of this might be similar to having employed the consultant in the first place, because many consultants need to use their own templates.

For around £500 + VAT, or less in US dollars, a business owner can purchase a CD containing templates for franchising a business. Be careful to find out who created the documents and ask in writing for confirmation that they own the full copyright. One franchisor using such a CD found she was unable to remove the references to the author's business, as he was really just trying to sell a copy of his franchise consultants' documentation. It was not only likely to be in breach of copyright, but contained details that were too specific for many other franchises and missed sections that many require.

The better CDs have a manual that discusses each section and gives ideas and suggestions about what should be included. It is worth looking at the company formation, data protection and tax sections to discover if it has been fully amended for a UK business.

Many more CDs are sold than completed, because it still requires the owner to have the time and commitment to work through the process. If the business owner could take a 4 or 6 week sabbatical and could look objectively at their business, this approach could be right for them.

If you are creating your own franchise package, you should set clear aims and goals, both for the existing business and the new franchised operation.

## Franchises work

There is one simple reason that franchises are so successful, which is that franchisees are legally bound to run their business in a prescribed way. Most people starting a business deviate from their plans. Often they do not have a clear idea of what they should be doing on any given day and many are learning as they go. Contrast that to a new business that has branded marketing, a large detailed operational manual and a requirement to follow steps that have be proven to work.

Many businesses would improve their profitability, and therefore be more attractive to prospective franchisees, if they had an Operations Manual created for them, and their management team insisted it was followed. Add to this by setting clear objectives with timelines and goals and you will be following in the footsteps of thriving franchised businesses.

Business expansion, including franchising, requires a commitment from the owner and often key members of their staff. It is therefore vital that the business owner watches the key indicators of the core business during the franchising process. They need to be alert to anything that shows fading results, which could be due to the business's management focusing on growth. If business performance drops, it will be much more difficult to sell the franchises. Conversely if the business is showing a growth spurt, franchisees will look at it more positively.

It is therefore just as important to have written plans for the core business, as it is for the franchisee. For the business the plans should allocate time and resources for both running the business and dealing with the franchising process. Time invested in the franchising process will be repaid as the business will have the tools to repeat a set expansion process over and over.

If a consultant is appointed they should provide a franchising feasibility study or a section in the Franchising Business Manual that incorporates the key elements of the above plans.

## Franchising is not a miracle cure

Most franchise consultants will tell you one of the most common reasons why a business owner contacts them is because their business is not making money. When asked, "Why do you think someone would wish to start up a branch of a loss-making business?", the answers follow the pattern below:

- I have never had the time to focus on the business
- I am not good at selling or marketing
- I have commitments so cannot open at the weekends
- My costs are too high, but if I could share them around a number of franchisees it would help.

If a business owner has a unique or novel business that is not making sufficient profits to franchise, there are investors than might purchase the business with the view to franchising it themselves. However, they will normally only pay for the value of the business today, not the value they will add by making it successful.

## Traits of a successful franchisor

It is important that the business owner considers the expansion options before selecting franchising. Often successful franchisors will fall into one of the following categories.

- A business owner wishes to expand and is willing to share the income and extra profit from the new operations in return for a lower investment than required for most organic expansion.

- The owner desires to share their skills and expertise with other business owners, who in return will support the owner and the brand.

- The owner has worked hard to build their business and has really enjoyed running it. They now wish to help others to set up their own business/make their dream come true, whilst, of course, increasing their income as payment.

- A business owner wishes to expand and is willing to invest in their business, but they do not have the financial resources to do it alone. Therefore they would rather support franchisees than either be dependent on a bank or sell part of their business to an investor.

- For some business owners, particularly those providing hands-on service work, e.g. cleaning, franchising gives them an opportunity to become a manager and trainer whilst taking a step away from the day-to-day provision of services.

- Retirement or exit planning has led the business owners to decide to build the business and prepare it for sale. With franchising, they can increase the value and demonstrate the growth potential in three years. It will also build their brand adding further value.

# Franchise types

It is important that the business owner clarifies the type of franchise they wish to operate before starting to create the franchise plans and documentation.

### Single branch franchise

This is the most common type of franchise. The franchisee purchases the franchise licence which allows some exclusive right to a territory where they can trade as if they were a branch of your business.

### Variations on the single branch franchise

Most franchisees are full-time but there are a growing number of part-time opportunities. It might be that the franchise is designed to fit in with school hours or has specific times the service can be delivered e.g. an after-school teaching franchise. Another example might be where the franchise has been designed to offer a complementary service e.g. a company formation franchise, for accountants.

Some arrangements are less formal licensing agreements than full franchising. These are often designed to assist a business to quickly create a nationwide service capability or coverage. Often the franchisee is only referred work, as and when it is available, in their location.

Appointing franchise agents who dual brand their business can often be the best solution for creating a national network of sales outlets.

For example, John Smith's Tyres could sign an exclusive deal with a leading remould tyre business, UK Tyre Treads. He could still sell new tyres for other manufacturers, but would only repair tyres using UK Tyre Treads equipment and materials. He would then trade as both John Smiths Tyres and UK Tyre Treads. This is different to being an agent who could sell a variety of brands. The franchisee would have an exclusive area, whereas a reseller would be competing with other businesses locally.

**Multi branch franchisees**

A franchisee might purchase the adjoining territory to their own. This is most popular when a city is divided into two franchise territories.

In other cases, a franchisee might purchase a second franchise for a family member to run, but they still own the franchise.

The next step up is where the franchisee has their own branch and territory. They also provide the support and training for smaller franchisees located in their area. This arrangement works well where expensive equipment is required but the cost cannot be justified for smaller franchises. John Smith's Nationwide Gardening Service could require franchises to own a ride-on mower, a towable branch shedder and access platforms for cutting hedges. For a large franchisee this could make sense. For a small one-man franchise, the equipment might only be required when employing extra staff. The main area franchisee would provide the extra branded equipment and trained personnel.

**Master Franchise**

These mainly suit either investors or managers. The Master Franchisee will be allocated a large territory, sometimes a county, even a continent e.g. Europe, or a region. The franchisee would often operate the first franchise in their area, as part of their training and then as a training base for future franchisees. In effect they become a development partner for the franchisor. They sell franchises in their territory and retain a large proportion of the franchise fees. This works well in areas such as Asia, where each country has different rules and customs. Also, the master franchise will often handle the translation of the franchise documentation and, in partnership with the franchisor, tailor the franchise to that country.

## Selecting franchisees

Franchisees are often people whose first decision is that they wish to be their own boss. Many have been in employment, so will not have had experience of running a business. So they decide to purchase a franchise, as it is a much safer option and they are provided with training and support. Only then do they look around to see what franchises are available, which suit their budget and which they think they can do.

Branding and image can be very important to someone considering purchasing a franchise. Prospective franchisees are often trying to maintain or enhance their status, therefore they will select a franchise that has a brand image which matches their last employer's. They may not wish to purchase a franchise from a famous PLC, but they will want to look and feel good in their new role. Also, many start-up franchisees will look for financial support from their family, so again a business that looks professional and has smart materials helps them to enlist support.

The franchisor therefore should be open to all potential recruits, as some of the less likely applicants make great franchisees.

Selecting the correct people to become your first franchisee is very important. Successful franchisees are people who are happy to follow in the footsteps of a profitable business owner and like the idea of having the support and guidance that franchising should provide.

The potential franchisee has to be in a position to fund all or part of the franchise fee. Often if they can find 30%, they can borrow 70% over 5 or 10 years.

Another positive aspect of purchasing a franchise over starting a business is the speed that the new business owner can start to earn an income.

For those who are considering becoming self-employed because of redundancy, purchasing a franchise offers a much quicker route to starting a business than going it alone. Many of those franchisees who are still in employment can complete much of the business set-up, training and production of the marketing materials whilst they are working.

When setting up a new business, much of the preparation time is working on a business plan, finding suppliers, producing a brand and marketing materials, plus much more. With the franchise, not only are these items provided but they have also been tested.

This means in the month before launch many new franchisees have started pre-launch marketing, including building their social networks, creating email and mailing lists. Some will have even set up sales meetings and have sent out invites to the open-day launch. Therefore, when preparing a business to expand as a franchise, the business owner should build a quick launch into their systems.

Often, new business owners find they suddenly get hit with unexpected administration or other tasks, whereas the franchisees will have been trained in what to expect. The Operations Manual should provide a plan of how to use their time. So when creating a franchised business, focus on building a step-by-step business model for the franchisee, with a realistic timescale.

Many franchisors do not ask for the franchisees to have experience or skills in the trade, they are looking for prospective franchisees who are ready to be taught systems and the skill set that they require. There are franchises, e.g. MOT centres, where a qualification is required. However, with the range of part-time courses it is often surprising how quickly these qualifications can be obtained. The franchisors may be able to offer one month's work experience and provide their own qualifications at the end of the training. This can add to the value of the franchise or it could be a disincentive if the cost of being away from home and not earning for a month is taken into account.

More mature prospective franchisees are more likely to welcome the opportunity of retraining for a new career and might find it easier to fund this.

**A word of caution**

Business owners who are new to appointing franchisees really have to be careful. It makes sense to have someone with you when carrying out interviews. Give that person the role of judging if the prospective franchisee will keep to the systems and is the correct type of person for the franchise. This allows the business owner to focus on selling the franchise.

The business owner has to bear in mind that someone who wishes to be a free spirit might have issues with following a detailed operations manual. If potential recruits at an interview are suggesting ways they can help develop the business or discussing changes to the brand or systems, the franchisor should be doubly cautious. Franchises work because everyone copies a successful formula.

# Recruiting Franchisees

There is not a set way to promote and recruit franchisees. The skill is to identify the way that suits the business being franchised. If you are using a franchise consultant they should start by helping you define how to reach potential franchisees.

There are a number of points to consider, however starting with the acceptable geographic locations and the skills required by successful franchisees can narrow the options substantially.

For many franchisors it is easier if the new franchisee is close to their present business base. This makes training and support more manageable and hands-on. For most businesses expanding through becoming a franchisor, their brand and business will only be known locally. Therefore, marketing is easier and there are more joint marketing opportunities if the territories adjoin or are close by.

If a business owner is franchising with the aim of providing a national service from regional bases, rather than from their one head office, a wide geographical spread would be ideal. With this approach both franchisor and franchisee should be realistic about the travelling required for training and support.

Deciding the skills required to be successful as a franchisee for a particular business is a difficult task for business owners. Many start from the point that it takes many years, or at least months, to be good at whatever they do. The owner finds it hard to believe that a novice can be trained to carry out their high standards in weeks. A good franchise consultant or possibly a creator of training courses can provide valuable advice in this area.

The business owner has to make the prospectus attractive and complete. They should then check that both the printed materials and what they are saying is believable. For example, a prospectus may say, "Weekend trade is important, so shop windows have updated posters and are cleaned every Friday". If the prospective franchisee decides to look at the shop late on Friday and the poster is the same as the weekend before and the windows are not clean, they will doubt and start checking everything. Therefore as the Operations Manual is written, all staff and anyone involved has to be trained to follow it in detail. The owner has to manage this, because they are selling the rights for someone to copy their every step.

It is important to make the franchise offer attractive. Therefore do not speak in jargon that relates to specific trades because all potential franchisees need to feel comfortable. It is often the prospective franchisee who says very little at the first meeting who becomes the best one in the long-term. They have so much to take in on their first meeting. It is important that the business owner remembers that it has taken years for them to know the business backwards.

Once the business owner has drafted their recruitment materials and has their operations manual in place, they need to be absolutely clear about the type of franchise they are offering. Most will start with Single branch franchises. The owner has to manage this and avoid the temptation of thinking, "let's see who shows an interest and then we can mould the franchise to fit". Franchises work because a tried and tested route is followed. If someone cannot define the franchise they are going to sell, how can they define the step-by-step processes?

Before advertising or promoting a franchise, the new franchisor should consider how they will train new franchisees and provide on-going management. Training and support is a critical component when promoting and selling a franchise and one of the items that will make prospective franchisees decide to join a franchise or not.

# Marketing your franchise

The most common way to promote franchises are Franchise and Business Growth exhibitions, advertising in franchise magazines, listing on-line in franchise directories or Businesses for Sale and networking on and off-line.

These can add considerably to the cost of becoming a franchisor, so it is worth considering other ways to promote a franchise.

The sides of a van or a shop window can be a powerful advertising space. A poster saying "Be your own boss by running a branch of John Smith Tyres. £10,000 investment required - £3,000 cash and £7,000 loan, subject to status", gives people a chance to see your business in action.

For lower cost franchises in defined geographical areas, calling, emailing and mailing contacts such as business advisers, Prince's Trusts, bank managers and anyone providing employment or business start-up advice is a good way of spreading the word. Also, HR managers can be worth calling at a time they are making redundancies. If you support this with on-line promotion, including a dedicated web page, it will make your franchise seem more established.

For many trades there are publications that are read every week by the main target audience for the franchise. Also, there should be organisations for people who carry out that trade. One franchise consultant quotes a very successful lower cost recruitment example. He was franchising a lawn-care business set up by ex-golf club green keepers. When speaking to them they showed him a small black and white monthly publication that green keepers read to keep up to date with treatments, techniques and equipment. Placing adverts for green keepers who were hoping to be their own bosses, and giving them the opportunity to work with the support of other professional lawn experts, worked because it was targeted so precisely.

# BFA approval

To be able to apply for BFA (British Franchising Association) membership, the franchisor will be required to meet set criteria and pay the membership fee. The annual fee is over £2,500 and many franchisors will require assistance with their application and incur costs in providing proof they meet the BFA Criteria.

As with any commercial decision, the business owner has to consider the value of this membership. In fact, it might be required for franchisees that have a high franchise fee or those that require premises and bank lending. For smaller and service franchises, the business owner can often sell the first two franchises before they decide on membership. The owner needs to consider whether the £2,500 needed for BFA membership could be better spent on marketing.

Being able to display the BFA logo might assist in selling franchises however, the franchise still has to be advertised.

The BFA operate some of the franchising exhibitions where the franchise could be promoted to people attending to look such opportunities. The stands are for members only and the cost starts at circa £4,000. There will be other costs, from exhibition stands to overnight accommodation.

Other exhibitions are available for all franchisors, both nationally and regionally.

# Franchise documentation

Franchisor's Business Manual or Franchise Development Model (the latter used to be referred to as a Feasibility Study).

The above two documents start with the same process, however, the Franchisor's Business Manual, is a document for on-going use by the franchisor, in much the same ways as the franchisee has their manual. The main difference is the Franchise Business Manual covers recruitment, details of what is contained in the legal agreement, and how to support the franchisees. It is a document that should be developed alongside the Operations Manual. Here we have covered them separately.

## Franchise Development Model or Feasibility Study.

The exact format and order the information is arranged in depends on who produces the document. The key sections are:

- The relevant history and the owner's philosophy of the business
- An overview of the business once it has become a franchisor.
- The branding, Intellectual Property (IP) and business's position in the market place before and after franchising

- Statistics and comments designed to prove the proposed business model is suitable for franchising. Demand for the franchise from prospective franchisees.

The process of proving the above will be on the basis of comparing the earnings of the business to average wages for that trade or the projected income from similar franchises. The key to proving profitability are the figures in the published and management accounts.

The document will then demonstrate there is a demand for the product or service. Again, it will use the trading experience and that of similar businesses. Where a service is unique, the business performance will be the main key. It will show how the business will be presented in an attractive way, to the appropriate prospective franchisees. The conclusion will be, if the above is true, the business will be a realistic franchise prospect.

The above is an important part of establishing credibility and parts of it will be repeated in the recruitment documents. In short, it will add weight to your view that the business is suitable for franchising and franchisees should make an adequate ROI.

This section would be followed by two sets of tables. The first relates to the franchised business and the second to the franchisees:

Set-up costs

Projected sales with appropriate cost of sales

P&L for 2 or 3 years for the franchisor and the term of the franchise agreement, for the franchisee.

Details or overview of the territories

For the franchisee only, there should be minimum performance criteria (sales or income) they must achieve.

Much of the remainder of the document will be general information on franchising and cover the subjects in the book in greater detail. Other books and ebooks also contain this information, many in great detail.

**Franchisor's Business Manual**

This document will contain all the information that relates to the business that is being franchised, including the subjects covered in the Franchise Development Model above.

It also details tasks, processes and how to support franchisees. Many of the more traditional franchise development models deal with how to set up the franchise and recruit the first franchisees, but do not give the franchise owner details of the on-going support they need to provide. The Franchise Business Manual will detail any changes required to the core business. It will detail the recruitment process, whereas the Franchise Development Model contains this information in a separate Recruitment Manual.

**Franchisee's Operations Manual**

This document should be designed for daily use by both the franchisee and the franchisor. It must cover all aspects of the business, from what to do each day, to using the business system and generally how to run the franchise.

Many of the newer manuals separate how to set up the franchise and run it in the early days from the information required by an established franchisee. This approach can make the manual much more user friendly and relevant to the franchisee.

Start up:

- Overview of the business and philosophy of the business owner
- How to establish the business and legal structure

- How to open accounts and take out insurance
- Time lines and milestones, with a plan of how to achieve these
- How to set up premises, equipment and other infrastructure
- How to set targets and initiate reporting system
- The launch, marketing, branding and how to make sales
- How to run a business and maintain complete business records.

The on-going sections of the manual will be:

- How to complete all everyday procedures and tasks
- How to market the business, increase the customer base and carry out the sales process
- When and how to report
- End of month and year reporting.
- Operating the business, updating targets and business development
- How to operate business systems including stock control, purchasing, manufacturing, customer service and IT systems.

**Recruitment Manual** – this is included in the Franchisor's Business Manual, where used.

The recruitment manuals vary greatly, depending on who writes them. Some follow the 'How to market' general books. Others tailor these to include just the methods being used to promote the franchise. Generally it will suggest that a set sum is allowed for marketing, per month.

Another type starts with a fairly detailed Marketing Plan. As they are detailed they can have actual budgets both for expenditure and response. The advantage of this type of plan is that there is a timed task list, which follows the same pattern as the other manuals.

All of the above recruitment models contain examples of documents required in the recruitment process. Some include samples of other businesses' recruitment brochures. On-line listings, social networks, email marketing and a recruitment website should be included as these extend the value of the marketing budget.

Most recruitment manuals include a section on the process of interviewing and appointing franchisees.

## Franchise Disclosure Document and Non-Disclosure Documents

All franchise consultants will include these either as a standalone document or contained within one of the documents listed above. The Franchise Disclosure Document lists the key points that the franchisee must be informed of, to make a fair decision on whether to enter into a franchise agreement with the franchisor. In the USA these are often hundreds of pages long and are created by a franchise attorney. The Franchise Disclosure Document is similar to the prospectuses that are issued when a business goes public. Many people will only have seen one when their building society converted from a mutual company to a PLC. In the UK most franchises list the key points that are contained in the legal agreement, operations manual and recruitment materials.

## Legal agreement

Franchise consultants can assist you in creating a brief for the franchise solicitor. The solicitor will also wish to see the FDD (Franchise Disclosure Document), the Operations Manual and the recruitment materials. Their role is to create a document that protects the franchisor's brand, the core business and the investment of other franchisees. It also allows to franchisor to take appropriate action to force a franchisee to follow the steps laid out in the Operational Manuals. The agreement will deal with early termination, either by agreement or for breach of the terms.

Franchisors selecting the DIY or CD option are likely to have a draft legal agreement in any pack of templates they purchase. Firstly, make sure it is an English template; the rules governing franchises are very different in the US and in some other counties. If an unqualified person produces the Legal Agreement, there are risks. The court's interpretation of one or more clause might be quite different to what you expect. Make sure your terms are balanced and reasonable. If you take this approach, do so with open eyes.

**The stages of franchising a business**

The process is similar whether a franchise consultant is employed or if the business owner decides to create the franchise model and documentation themselves. The questions still have to be asked, decisions have to be made and the time consuming documentation has to be produced.

## Start at the beginning

The business owner needs to take the time to consider the possible ways to expand the business. Create a list for each option, comparing the time and finance required against the projected income and future value of the business.

If the owner is considering employing a franchise consultant, ask for their views, general comments and general expected return on investment. Most consultants should provide this free, in return for being able to provide you with a quotation for handling some or all of the process.

**Meeting between business owner and selected franchise consultant/adviser to discuss:**

- The suitability of franchising for this particular business
- The franchising type
- Changes to the business, its systems and processes, to simplify franchising
- Basic franchise model and what is being included
- Costs of franchising, including legal and IP (Intellectual Property)
- Timetable and the amount of time the business owner is required to commit.

Agree consultancy fees and total budget.

Sign agreement.

Agree start date.

**Fact finding**

The tone of this meeting might be different, because the consultant will not be selling and the business owner will not be purchasing and demonstrating their success. It is vital that whoever is producing the franchise model and package of documents has all the information available. This information is likely to include:

- Copies of the last three year's accounts and access to management accounts
- Access to, or copies of, all documents, forms, manuals, marketing materials that the business uses
- Information that might affect the franchised business that was not disclosed earlier
- Access to watch the business in action and ask staff questions about their role and the time it takes to carry out a task or the order that tasks have to be completed in. Also giving them the opportunity to make

suggestions of other ways tasks can be handled.
- Details of equipment and supplies used in the business.

From the above information and subsequent meetings and telephone calls the consultant or business owner has to produce.

- Franchisor's Business Manual or Franchise Development Model
- Franchisee's Operations Manual
- Recruitment Manual
- Franchisee agreement key points.

The business owner must allow time to read and approve the above documents and have time to answer questions that arise during the creation of these documents.

**Protecting your brand - Trademarks and Intellectual Properties**

The business owner cannot sell or licence a business unless you can prove ownership. Therefore registering trademarks, names and designs will need to be completed. Some consultants handle this, some business owners complete the process on-line and others employ an IP consultant.

This service is seldom included in the franchise consultant's quotation.

**Legal Agreement**

This part of the franchise development package should not be started until the documentation is complete and approved, as the legal agreement has to reflect the Operations Manual.

The cost of having a solicitor create a Legal Agreement is seldom included in the franchise consultant's quotation.

**Market, recruit and train franchisees**

This role will mainly be carried out by the business owner, using the plan in the agreed Recruitment Manual. Some franchise consultants will assist with marketing of the franchise or the business owner can employ a marketing company to handle or assist with the promotion.

Most business owners will carry out the training of the franchisees, but for those that are uncomfortable in that role, local trainers will be needed to work alongside the owner.

This service is seldom included in the franchise consultant's quotation.

**Provide on-going support**

To make a franchise successful, the franchisor should have regular contact with the franchisee. The skill is to keep the franchisee motivated, make them efficient and productive by following the Operations Manual and use the training to add extra services. This has to be balanced with making sure the franchisee promotes your business, runs it professionally and follows the manual to the letter.

## Now you can make it happen

Franchise your business and get other people to invest in building your brand.

In short you can punch above your weight – but it will take effort and commitment

Most businesses in the UK do not expand by becoming a franchisor only because they never thought of it. Read this straightforward guide so you are not just another business owner that misses a great expansion opportunity.

One misconception is that franchise consultants will make the franchise business model complicated. In fact, the opposite is normally true, a franchise consultant will be persuading the business owner to include less, make the business easier to operate and simpler to understand.

They will look for 'extras' that can be offered during the life of the franchise agreement, which will demonstrate to the franchisee that the franchisor is helping them to expand their business. It is marketing companies that always suggest adding more services to the franchise, to make it more attractive. This might achieve a greater number of leads, but it is likely to put off the ideal candidates who wish to be their own boss, but have a manageable first business.

**This page has been left blank for you to write down any questions you still may have about franchsing.**

**This page has been left blank for you to write down action you may be to take before you franchise your business.**

This page has been left blank for you to write down any other notes.

**Ian Stirling profile can be found on**

www.linkedin.com/in/ianstirling

**Tweet coments welcomed on**

www.twitter.com/ianstirling

**Objectives Reached**

www.objectivesreached.co.uk/franchising

www.ingramcontent.com/pod-product-compliance
Lightning Source LLC
Chambersburg PA
CBHW072250170526
45158CB00003BA/1047